D is for Drinking Gourd

An African American Alphabet

Written by Nancy I. Sanders and Illustrated by E. B. Lewis

Sleeping Bear Press™

310 North Main Street, Suite 300
Chelsea, MI 48118
www.sleepingbearpress.com

THOMSON
GALE

© 2007 Thomson Gale, a part of the Thomson Corporation.

Thomson, Star Logo and Sleeping Bear Press are trademarks
and Gale is a registered trademark used herein under license.

Printed and bound in China.

10 9 8 7 6 5 4 3 2 1

Library of Congress Cataloging-in-Publication Data

Sanders, Nancy I.
D is for drinking gourd : an African American alphabet / written by
Nancy I. Sanders ; illustrated by E. B. Lewis.
p. cm.
Summary: "Using the alphabet to introduce its contents, this book
includes topic such as abolitionists, cowboys, Harlem Renaissance, and
Kwanzaa"—Provided by publisher.
ISBN 13: 978-1-58536-293-6
1. African Americans—Juvenile literature. 2. English
language—Alphabet—Juvenile literature. I. Lewis, Earl B. II. Title.
E185.S17 2007
973'.0496073003—dc22   2007005462

God bless our native land,
Land of the newly free,
Oh may she ever stand
For truth and liberty.

from *God Bless Our Native Land*
by Frances E. W. Harper

"Let our people go!" they cried
          in speeches or with pen in hand.
A is for abolitionists
    who were willing to take a stand.

In the years before the Civil War, abolitionists were a group of people who tried to bring slavery to an end. Men and women traveled throughout the states speaking against the evils of slavery. A strong woman of faith and a former slave, Sojourner Truth was a powerful speaker in support of abolition and women's rights. Frederick Douglass escaped from bondage to become one of the most important abolitionist leaders. His autobiography caused many others to understand what slavery was really like. Journalist, doctor, explorer, and leading abolitionist who frequently spoke with Douglass, Martin Delany was appointed as a major in the Union Army during the Civil War.

The black press, newspapers owned and operated by African Americans, printed numerous articles challenging fellow Americans to join together in the fight against slavery. The most famous newspaper of all, *The North Star*, was co-edited by Frederick Douglass and Martin Delany.

After the Civil War, African American soldiers were stationed on the western frontier. The Native Americans gave them the honorable nickname of "Buffalo Soldiers."

When the U.S. government treated Native Americans unfairly in attempting to take over and settle their land, various tribes responded by attacking wagon trains, settlers, stagecoaches, and trains. Both the Infantry and Cavalry units of Buffalo Soldiers were called out to offer protection from these attacks. More than a dozen men were awarded the Congressional Medal of Honor.

To test bicycles for military use, in 1897 the 25th Infantry rode bicycles from Montana to St. Louis, Missouri. As these Buffalo Soldiers traveled through the countryside, onlookers gathered to cheer them on.

B is for Buffalo Soldiers
riding across the plains.
Bold and brave, they protected the West—
the settlers, the forts, and the trains.

C c

Sweat-stained hats and spurs that jingled,
rodeos with daredevil clowns,
C is for the cowboys
and cattle drives to railroad towns.

During the late 1800s, more than 5,000 black cowboys rode the Chisholm Trail, driving cattle from Texas north to the railroad in Abilene, Kansas.

Rodeo stars such as Nat Love and Bill Pickett drew huge crowds. Love was well known for his keen sharpshooting abilities. Pickett was famous for his technique known as bulldogging where he bit a steer on the muzzle and wrestled it to the ground. Pickett was the first African American admitted to the National Rodeo Cowboy Hall of Fame.

Marshall Bass Reeves kept law and order throughout the West. Wearing disguises and speaking several Native American languages, he brought over 3,000 outlaws to justice during the 32 years he served as Deputy U.S. Marshal in the Indian Territory.

Numerous African Americans settled in the wild, Wild West. Encouraged by Benjamin "Pap" Singleton, thousands of families left the South in 1879. Many established all-black towns in Kansas. These pioneers, cowboys, and settlers were known as Exodusters.

The Big Dipper was commonly called the Drinking Gourd because it reminded people of the dry gourds they used to dip water out of a bucket for a drink. At night, fugitive slaves looked up at the Drinking Gourd to locate the North Star. The North Star helped guide them to the northern states where they would be free.

Men and women known as "conductors" often hid runaways in their homes along a secret route called the Underground Railroad. People such as William Still, David Ruggles, and William Whipper used their own money to help hundreds escape north. Harriet Tubman, or Moses as some called her, journeyed deep into the southern states. She personally led over 300 slaves to freedom.

Spirituals and songs such as "Follow the Drinking Gourd" often contained secret codes to pass important information from one person to the next about escaping on the Underground Railroad.

D is for Drinking Gourd,
    and the North Star that led through the night
from station to station on the Underground Railroad,
    escaping on a dangerous flight.

E e

E is for Emancipation,
a big word that means to be free.
When people heard the proclamation,
it was a day of jubilee!

On January 1, 1863, President Lincoln issued the Emancipation Proclamation. This important document officially freed all the slaves in the southern states. Many referred to this as the day of jubilee because great rejoicing took place.

The news did not reach Texas until more than two years later. On June 19, 1865, General Granger rode into Galveston, Texas and read the Emancipation Proclamation aloud for all to hear. A great celebration was held.

Juneteenth is a special holiday held each year in June to remember the historic day emancipation was brought to Texas. Friends and families gather to celebrate with festivals and parades all across America.

There were more than 5,000 black patriots fighting for independence in the American Revolution. African Americans fought in every major battle of the war.

Crispus Attucks, the first person to die in the fight for liberty, was killed during the Boston Massacre. Prince Estabrook and Peter Salem were minutemen at Lexington and Concord when the first shots were fired.

The early American government did not allow men of color to participate as political leaders, so there were no signatures of African Americans on the Declaration of Independence. Richard Allen, Absalom Jones, and James Forten, however, met just down the street from Independence Hall in Philadelphia, the new nation's capital. These Founding Fathers organized free blacks, and founded numerous societies and churches. Their tireless efforts helped bring an end to the slave trade and eventually slavery itself.

Just before the U.S. Constitution was written, Richard Allen and Absalom Jones organized the Free African Society to help the poor, promote justice, and provide a place to worship. Because it was the first organization of its kind for African Americans, this society was a monumental step in the history of America.

Ff

F is for our Founding Fathers
in the days of the Constitution.
They helped win the war from British rule
in the American Revolution.

G g

That's why **G** is for Great Migration.

Thousands moved from the South to the North. Families went to the cities looking for jobs and a better education.

When World War I began, America's doors closed to the arrival of European immigrants. At the same time, northern industries needed more workers to produce manufactured goods for the war. Industries advertised throughout the South, inviting African Americans to move to northern cities such as Pittsburgh and Chicago.

Because of the increase of violence against African Americans, the South had become a very dangerous place to stay. Also, segregation laws in southern states made life unbearable, taking away voting privileges, educational opportunities, and equal rights. Entire black communities packed their bags and moved north.

Many societies, such as the National Urban League, were formed to help family members find a place to stay, get a job, and adjust to their new surroundings.

Nannie Helen Burroughs believed that education was the key to a successful future. She established the National Training School for Women and Girls in Washington, D.C., and was an influential leader in many societies and clubs.

H h

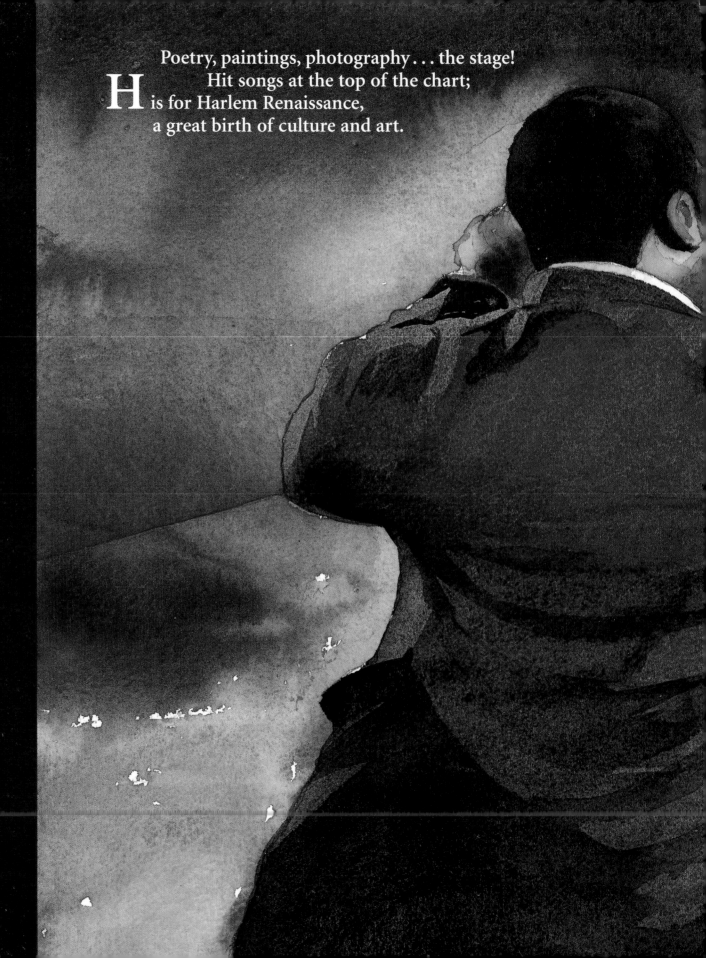

Poetry, paintings, photography... the stage!
Hit songs at the top of the chart;
H is for Harlem Renaissance,
a great birth of culture and art.

People flocked to Harlem in the 1920s. Artists, writers, musicians, and political activists gathered in this New York neighborhood to express their ideas.

Langston Hughes, one of the most famous writers of all time, is known as the poet laureate of Harlem.

Among her other writings, Zora Neale Hurston wrote down collections of folk tales that reveal what life was like living in the South.

An outstanding student, athlete, singer, and activist for civil rights, Paul Robeson chose a career in acting. His starring role in the stage performance of *Othello* won him great fame.

Known as the Empress of the Blues, Bessie Smith captivated audiences with her rich voice and unique style of singing.

Augusta Savage was a famous sculptor whose work included lifelike portraits of African American heroes.

As a photographer, James VanDerZee captured the Harlem Renaissance on film.

There have been many inventions made by African Americans. Norbert Rillieux invented a better process for making sugar. Elijah McCoy invented a machine to oil engines on trains and ships. Jan Ernst Matzeliger invented a machine that made it easier to manufacture shoes. Lewis Latimer invented a better filament to be used in lightbulbs. A self-made millionaire, Madam C. J. Walker invented hair products and beauty creams.

Modern inventions include the Super Soaker, a popular squirt gun invented by Lonnie Johnson. Kenneth Dunkley invented the Three-Dimensional Viewing Glasses, which make it possible for readers to view an ordinary magazine in stunning 3-D. Scientists and engineers are constantly working on new inventions such as Thomas Mensah's fiber optics research, James McLurkin's micro-robots design, and Patricia Bath's invention of a tool that uses a laser to treat blindness.

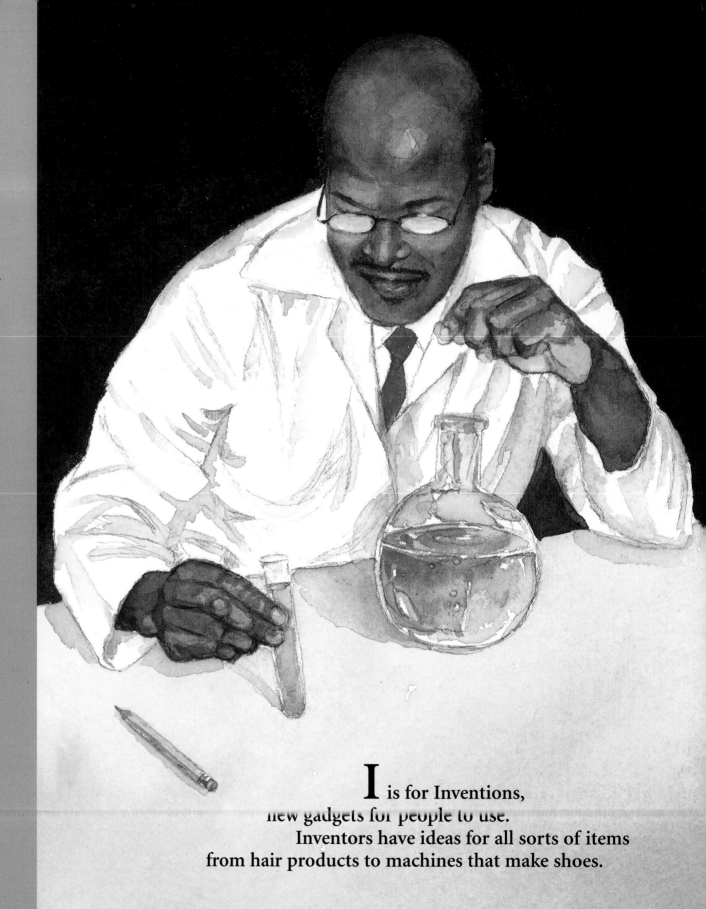

I is for Inventions,
new gadgets for people to use.
Inventors have ideas for all sorts of items
from hair products to machines that make shoes.

J j

Trumpets playing to a syncopated beat,
crowds forming just to hear,
J is for Jazz and jazz musician.
There's a new song in the air!

Louis Armstrong was known by his many fans as "Satchmo." A genius with his trumpet, Armstrong was also world famous for his rich, deep voice. He was the most important soloist in the history of jazz.

Duke Ellington and his band brought jazz into the hearts and homes of America. Through radio shows, live performances, and recordings, millions listened to the songs Ellington wrote, played, and directed.

One of the greatest voices in jazz, Ella Fitzgerald won many honors and awards.

Sarah Vaughan's amazing vocal range and singing ability won her the nickname, "Divine One."

Born in New Orleans, Wynton Marsalis uses his trumpet to bring jazz to audiences today. Through television and workshops, Marsalis also teaches about the history of jazz. He is co-founder and artistic director of a program in New York City called Jazz at Lincoln Center.

Lighting candles, telling stories,
reciting an inspirational quote;
K is for Kwanzaa,
a celebration of unity and hope.

Family and friends gather to celebrate Kwanzaa, a holiday that lasts from December 26 through January 1.

Developed by Maulana Karenga in 1966, the word Kwanzaa means "first fruits" in Swahili.

The seven principles of Kwanzaa are unity, self-determination, collective work and responsibility, cooperative economics, purpose, creativity, and faith.

The seven symbols of Kwanzaa are fruits, vegetables, and nuts; a placemat; a candle-holder; ears of corn; gifts; the cup of unity; and seven candles.

Kwanzaa is a time to celebrate important achievements by African Americans. There have been numerous accomplishments throughout the years, especially in the world of science and medicine. Scientist George Washington Carver invented an amazing variety of products from crops such as sweet potatoes and peanuts. Biologist Ernest E. Just discovered important information about how cells work. Dr. Charles Drew conducted extensive research on blood, making success-ful blood banks possible in hospitals today. Dr. Jane Wright and her father, Dr. Louis Wright, were pioneers in cancer research.

Kk

L is for Little Rock Nine,
the students who integrated school
at Little Rock, Arkansas's, Central High—
protected under military rule.

Before the 1960s, many schools in the southern states were segregated. This meant that black children could not attend the same schools as white children.

In 1957 the Little Rock school board offered permission for families to integrate their children into the local high school. Dorothy Bates, leader of the National Association for the Advancement of Colored People (NAACP), volunteered to help. Against great opposition and many threats of violence, nine high school students bravely tried to attend the all-white Central High School in Little Rock, Arkansas. When the governor of Arkansas refused to allow them to enroll, President Dwight D. Eisenhower ordered federal troops to step in. The heroic young women and men were able to attend school with soldiers by their side, offering military protection and support.

The nine courageous students who integrated Central High School were Minni-Jean Brown, Elizabeth Eckford, Ernest Green, Thelma Mothershed, Melba Patillo, Gloria Ray, Terrance Roberts, Jefferson Thomas, and Carlotta Walls.

Ll

M m

M is for March on Washington,
a civil rights demonstration
where thousands of people gathered to support
equal rights throughout the nation.

On August 28, 1963, nearly 250,000 people gathered in Washington, D.C. to support civil rights and the end of segregation. This demonstration helped influence Congress to pass President John F. Kennedy's Civil Rights Act. People from all across the U.S. gathered at the Washington Monument and marched peacefully to the Lincoln Memorial where prayers, songs, and speeches were heard.

The most famous speech that day was "I Have a Dream" by Dr. Martin Luther King Jr. A strong supporter of nonviolent action, Dr. King was president of the Southern Christian Leadership Conference (SCLC). Pastor of the Dexter Avenue Baptist Church in Montgomery, Alabama, Dr. King led numerous marches and crusades in support of equal rights, including the famous children's march and the Montgomery Bus Boycott, sparked when Rosa Parks was arrested because she refused to move to the back of the bus. Dr. King was awarded the Nobel Peace Prize in 1964. In 1968 people all around the world mourned when they heard the shocking news that he had been assassinated.

N is for NAACP
and the legal help it provides.
This important organization
has saved countless numbers of lives.

Formed in 1909, the National Association for the Advancement of Colored People (NAACP) has been a powerful voice in legal victories, educational opportunities, economic improvement, and civil rights. Its lawyers have worked hard in successful court battles to protect people from injustices such as mob violence, false accusations, and racial discrimination.

W. E. B. Du Bois was among the founding members of the NAACP. An outstanding scholar, important historian, and monumental leader, he dedicated most of his life to the pursuit of equal rights in America.

The Crisis was the official journal of the NAACP. As its editor, Du Bois featured news updates and published a variety of works by Harlem Renaissance writers.

Thurgood Marshall was a lawyer for the NAACP who won many landmark court cases. In 1967 he became the first African American justice of the Supreme Court of the United States.

Outstanding athletes each do their best,
inspiring both young and old.
O is for Olympic medals—
the bronze, the silver, the gold.

Athletes set amazing Olympic records in track and field. In 1936 Jesse Owens was the star of the Berlin Olympics. He raced to victory after victory, winning four gold medals. Nearly 50 years later, Carl Lewis followed in Owens' footsteps to win four gold medals in the 1984 Olympics. Competing over several Olympics, Jackie Joyner-Kersee won bronze, silver, and gold medals for a total of six in all.

Muhammad Ali was one of many boxers who won the gold medal.

Gymnast Dominique Dawes and ice skater Debra Thomas each won medals for outstanding performance and skill.

Champions such as Bill Russell, Cheryl Miller, Earvin "Magic" Johnson, and Michael Jordan joined their Olympic teams for thrilling performances on the basketball court.

In 2002 a new star was born! Vonetta Flowers sped down snowy slopes to a surprising victory in a bright red bobsled with her racing partner, Jill Bakken. Flowers became the first African American to win a gold medal in the Winter Olympics.

Pp

Government leaders make important decisions for people in their cities and states. P is for Politics and politicians and political candidates.

Many African American men and women have been elected as mayors, governors, senators, and other political officials.

Hiram Revels and Blanche Bruce became the first African Americans to serve in the United States Senate. They were elected during Reconstruction, a short period of time after the Civil War when hundreds of African Americans were elected to government positions throughout the South.

One of the most influential members of President Franklin Roosevelt's Black Cabinet was Mary McLeod Bethune, who was also the advisor of several other presidents. The Black Cabinet gave advice to the president about how to help African Americans get better housing, food, and jobs.

His popularity and enthusiasm brought Barack Obama to center stage in the political arena with his 2004 election to the United States Senate. He is the fifth African American to serve in the Senate, following in the footsteps of such political leaders as Hiram Revels, Blanche Bruce, Edward Brooke, and Carol Moseley Braun.

Colin Powell and Condaleeza Rice became two of the most important government officials in America. During the years George W. Bush was president, each was appointed secretary of state.